D1329773

THINGS MY MOTHER LEFT BEHIND

Susan Richardson

Susan Richardson

https://floweringink.com

First Printing: July 2020

Potter's Grove Press, LLC

https://pottersgrovepress.com

ISBN-978-1-951840-11-2

~For my Mom and Dad, who gave me music and poetry, and for Joe who sees me in light and in darkness~

FOREWORD

by

Bojana Stojčić, writer

In an attempt to best describe Susan Richardson's poetry, and a world where "everything is so quiet and so very loud," I once paraphrased Nietzsche who called himself a forest, and a night of dark trees. There is nothing light about her poetry, and nothing fake either. It is brutally honest and hauntingly beautiful, the spitting image of her darkness, if you will, and, finally, something to be embraced because if you stay clear of it, you will miss finding banks full of roses under her cypresses.

Susan describes herself as a writer and a poet, going blind in L.A. This collection of exquisite poems and musings shows us someone who is much more than that. It is a heartfelt "story of a slow approach to blindness" gripping her body and mind in a steely claw, a gut-wrenching confession about her past and present, where everything breaks her down to the bottle she wishes she could smash against the sky, and a painful monologue about loss, focusing on both her mother's early death, "leaving the weight of sorrow to darken my bones," and an attempt to come to terms with her fears as she slowly loses her father to dementia.

Susan is not only a highly emotional person, feeling things more deeply and responding more intensely, but also a remarkably skilled and passionate poet; hence, reading her becomes a visceral experience. The imagery she selflessly uses is as a rule complex, appealing to all our senses. In her work, we see a knot in the pit of her stomach and "rage weaving into the air around her," we taste her bitter defeats in our mouth, we feel the burden of her tears, hear her ear-splitting storms, "the clamor of her rain," and smell her escapes.

In her poems, she gives the reader everything – her flesh, her blood, "the sounds of suffering," and the fury "blooming in the back of my throat." Her vulnerability, so raw, it goes beneath your skin. She suggests in a couple of verses/paragraphs what could not be stated in a volume. Such is the quality of Susan's words. She is her voice – relentlessly authentic and unforgettable – which cannot be overshadowed by wells or walls for in her fragility lies her greatest strength.

Susan Richardson is not a poet of the moment, nor will her work discover depths of meaning in everyday life. It is rather a personal journey into the very heart of darkness, and the road less traveled she does take, despite seeing it as pointless more often than not. Ultimately, however "heavy and uncertain" her steps may be, however indisposed we might find her while grieving her wounds and disappointments, however furious for failing herself and her loved ones, she does not invite us to a pity party, knowing "it is futile; this hiding." Instead, she gives us her eyes and lets us join her on the long path to self-discovery, along which she hopes to "stitch pieces back into place" and by the end of which, if lucky, we will all learn to see.

CONTENTS

FROM WAVES

I am from the bones of peasants
From the depth of emeralds and glasses of whiskey
I am from the throats of storytellers
and coal miners buried in the roots of trees
I am from guitar strings that pay homage to
hurricanes raging in bellies of lead
From piano keys and jazz riffs winding
into the mouths of sleeping villages

I come from the waves
Born into battle, too small and too soon
From fragments and the failure to fix a marriage
broken by deceit
I am from sadness nestled in the arms of sea spray
Witness to the sorrows of unrequited identity

I am from a maze of unraveling threads
and latch keys hidden in the beds of snapdragons
I am from holidays divided
Every other weekend and dinner on Wednesdays
I am from tumbling down sand dunes
Swan dives and death drops and somersaults over
shards of glass
I am from hours underwater

THINGS MY MOTHER LEFT BEHIND

Believing in mermaids and rising from the deep end

I am from white-glove tests covered in blood
China dolls shattered by rage and disease
I am from coming unhinged
and falling into bottles of booze
From Prozac and Xanax and the art of escape

I am from the love song of a madwoman
who eats men like air
From magic ignited
in the kitchen of a bonesetters daughter
I am from the fabric of language
The pulse of words
woven into what it means to feel alive

I am from climbing out of darkness
A rebellion, a roaring to stand and be heard
I am from true love the second time around
Sleuthing and laughter and sharing scars
I am from the discovery of hope
From seeing through blindness and finding a voice

A DRESS TO DIE IN

When she was 40, she dressed in vintage clothes,
patterns from the jazz age traversing over her shoulders.
She'd go to the local pizza joint for a slice of pepperoni,
sweeping through the door in a flourish of silk
and velvet, ensconced in a feathered cloche,
throat wrapped in emeralds.
Grand entrances were her thing.

At 48, when cancer thread itself into her breast
and chemotherapy loomed at the door
with teeth that threatened to break her,
she scoffed and went shopping
for what she called chemo clothes.
She arrived for her first appointment,
dazzling in a purple suede dress
adorned by costume jewelry with beads
the size of plumbs,
standing defiantly on platform heels,
ready to fight for her life.

In a hospital bed at 52, she scoured clothing catalogues
given to her in secret by night shift nurses,
and bought a dress to die in.
It was the shade of a young peach,

brushing light onto her cheeks,

soothing and softening the scent of illness on her skin.

She wore it the night of her final Christmas,

laughing and beautiful,

even as pain coursed through her body

and her organs began to fail.

It took 3 days for her to die,

light fading into shallow breath,

grief weaving itself like a bruise into the sun.

Hours before she died, she lifted the oxygen mask

from her face to breathe on her own

for the very last time.

She departed under a veil of defiance,

pulling color from the sky,

leaving the weight of sorrow to darken my bones.

FRAIL

When the sun shines for too many days, I start to remember the ways that life creeps up and grabs me by the throat, dashing whatever lofty plans I may have conjured up. I was going to be more disciplined, write more, do the laundry more often, be a better person. I have imagined myself as so many things, believed myself to be so much more than I am. I have accepted illusion over reality, climbed into the sounds of myself breaking and shattering as if these were acts of bravery. I convinced myself it was strength, believed that I was strong, but my reflection shows a woman who is frail and swallowed up by shadows. Time and again, I am a disappointment to myself.

I have called myself a kind person because kindness is the only thing I believed gave me value, but I am not always kind. I have called myself a good friend, but I am not a good friend. I am the friend who disappears, who retreats from the world into selfish and silent spaces. I wanted to be a good wife, but how can I be a good wife when the weight of my existence is a burden? I have dreamed of being an equal, but how can I stand next to someone when my steps are always too small, too timid? I believed I was smart, but how can I be smart when I understand so little?

I deem the machinations of my mind defective, deceitful, and irreparably flawed. I tether myself to affliction, name my reality depression, but perhaps the threads that comprise the fabric of who I am have always been weak and frayed. Perhaps blindness is not only my physical affliction but my emotional and intellectual affliction as well.

I try to capture images and expression from the disappearing spaces I step into with abandon. I allow my breath to become a kind of silence that numbs the ache, to escape the shackles of who I am. I release the weight of my skin and fall into who I have always been, rather than who I think I am meant to be.
We all travel on paths that veer and rise and plummet. We all grab onto hope and search for love. We all wear masks. It is in the removing of those masks, in those moments of darkness when the truth of my frailty lays bare like a wound, that I see through my blindness and fear that without it, I am nothing.

LEAVES

Another hospital room,
another chair holding the weight of my sorrow.
His breath is almost soundless,
mouth open wide
as if inviting god into his lungs one last time.

His eyes flutter awake,
startled.
Is it my face he sees,
dulled by time,
or a face that once held the sun?

He smiles and strokes my fifty-year-old hand,
all the years drifting away.
The blues sit perched on his dry lips.
I am his child,
four years old singing Lead Belly
at the top of my tiny lungs.

I am a drop of his blood
spilling out onto the earth,
a fracture of his bones
stuck into the ground with paper spikes.
I am the tear from his eye,

heavy,
reluctant.

His hands are a whisper that tell a story,
a smattering of leaves on his palm,
fingers plucking at things only he can see,
my mother,
my brother,
both long dead.

I watch his chest barely rising,
each small breath
a forest of words trapped in the mist of his memory.
I wait for his stillness,
for the breaking pieces of his mind to be at rest.

He sits in my palm now,
softly,
frail like the wing of a sparrow.
He folds into shapes
so tiny
so quiet.

THINGS MY MOTHER LEFT BEHIND

She left her thumbprint behind my eye,

corrupted strands of DNA woven into my blood,

waiting to stain my life with darkness.

I was conceived to cover up a deception,

born into the hands of a sun made of paper,

but her lies left slashes

where shadows escaped and smudged out the light.

She left her imprint on my hands,

self-loathing scarred into my fingertips,

and taught me how to abuse my body.

I was a child with a woman's curves,

boobs so big, she said I could pose for playboy.

I learned to purge the weight of shame,

disappear into shapes that couldn't be seen.

She left her blueprint on the machinations

of my mind, a schematic of sorrow

warning me to keep my secrets

trapped in the confines of my mouth.

Rage bloomed in the back of my throat,

but my lips held the scent of petals.

Nice girls never shout.

She left her fingerprints on my adolescence,
gnarled by the roots of genetic predisposition.
While my classmates went to dances,
feeling the surge and sting of first love,
I spent hours in the cancer ward,
watching disease slice into her breath,
learning the meaning of loss.

She left her boot print in the pit of my throat,
plucked out my voice with her disappearing act.
Beneath a green canvas tent,
erected to protect mourners from the rain,
I broke into pieces at the mouth of her grave,
with only the brittle threads of grief
to stitch myself back together.

ROCK BOTTOM

I got my first taste of escape at twelve,
chipping away the layers of self-control
with a bottle of stolen wine.
I stumbled home beneath a spinning sky,
passed out on the floor and pissed myself,
while my best friend puked up her innocence
on icy bathroom tiles.
"Your friend could have died,"
my mom said,
hoping I would never take another drink.

Guilt could not dissuade me.

At fourteen, I developed a craving
for the errant burn of vodka,
a flame that tore the fragility from my tongue.
Hard liquor became the master of dulling my sadness,
loosening the binds of self-loathing.
I broke off pieces of myself to numb
the brutality of sorrow,
quickly learning the dialogue of hangovers.

The headaches could not dissuade me.

Tequila brazenly graced my pallet,
heralding the arrival of an unsweetened sixteen,
a drug humming through my veins,
enticing me onto the path of liquored up sex.
I became well acquainted with the art of sneaking
out of the tangle of a strange boy's arms,
reeling with practiced stealth
through the bleary maze of the morning after.

Shame could not dissuade me.

I painted the decades with a palette of shadows,
wallowing in the parched mouth of regret,
lips blistered by the aftermath of nights
blacked out by booze.
When the sun pulled penitence from my chest,
I swore fealty to a healthier way of living,
reached for the hand of sobriety,
slipped.
There were no signs of peril below,
no craggy grooves to warn me.

Rock bottom has no texture.

HUNGER

Big egos get aroused under a spotlight,
preening in the center like musk melon shuckers.
Those who hate the heat of their own skin
creep around the edges with expressions of sadness
glued in place like badges of honor.

Feeding frenzies erupt over a smattering of praise.
Sustenance for those acquainted with self- loathing.
A path to victory for the arrogant who sit poised
behind a gilded lens, mouths lathered in conceit.

We all wake up hungry, scrambling after morsels
of what we think will make us feel special,
devouring lies from vapid tongues
and seeking out attention for our wounds.

I display the shapes of my scars with words
that twist in the teeth of starving readers,
and call myself a writer.
If I say I am compelled to write, is it true,
or just a ruse to cover hollowness?

BAREFOOT

I remember when the apartment was crisp,
the scent of winter
pressing itself against the windows,
the clutter only in my mind.

I used to love the sound of thunder,
the roar that traveled through the sky,
until death rattled
and blemished the air.

My hands are brittle and broken
from scraping gloom off the walls,
reaching through the cracks of shadows,
desperate to feel the light against my fingertips.

My strife impales the floor,
saturated in the filth of agony
that shellacs the splintering wood,
grime so thick it can't be mopped away.

I never walk barefoot in my house.

RISING FROM SIBERIAN SOIL

War ravaged the fragility of her girlhood,
threw it into a sky alight with bombs
and burned up reverie like a paper doll.
She was six years old, stealing away after bedtime,
clinging to the hem of her mother's rough woolen skirt.

Quietly. We must not be seen.

She ran for a year, over cadaverous ground
and rocks that ate holes into her leather shoes.
Empty storehouses sheltered her from the
bullets of soldiers who hunted Jewish families.
With each step, she fought for her survival,
until she was captured and encased in ice.

She was one of seven prisoners locked inside
a freezing shack, given a thin grey blanket to share.
Their breaking bodies were fed
with bowls of watery soup made from potatoes
her parents pulled out of the icy Siberian soil,
fingers bruised and stained by exhaustion.
Guards with guns kept watch, as a storm of carnage
raged outside the splintering slats of confinement.

Two years later, she emerged from her incarceration,
looking out onto the landscape with eyes full of death
and the sound of gunfire scarred into her ears.
Clinging tightly to her young sister's hand,
she followed her mother into the wilderness,
leaving the vestiges of her childhood on the prison floor.

Now, in her 80's, my step mother sees the world
in familiar shades of devastation,
terror seeping onto the canvas of a country
she believed would protect her.
Mad men disseminate hatred over nations that weep,
and she is that child again,
frozen under the grip of a war that
swallows people whole.

HUNTED

I swallow the prickly echoes of my fear,
faltering at the mouth of a street that flickers.
Like prey, I wander into the camouflage of
a darkening landscape and grasp at slivers
of sun that taunt the vestiges of my vision.

Twilight slips into the corner of my eye

I am hunted by an affliction that creeps covertly
behind my eyes and chisels away the light,
a slithering hum that heralds the shattering moon.
The clamor surges against the sky,
spackling my sight with shards of darkness.

Nightfall eclipses the shape of my eye

I stagger through narrowing doorways,
passages littered with veiled figures
and curves that send me careening into
the serrated throats of tripwires.
I fall at the feet of a malady that has no face.

Blindness takes root behind my eye

FALLING

Each time my father falls,
each time I fail to catch him,
patches of the sun grow dark.

Is this what he felt like, watching me fall,
keeping his arms pinned to his sides,
as he waited for his little girl
to pick herself up,
so he could mend her scraped knees?

It is my turn now,
to soothe the bruises of his winter,
weave comfort through the haze that seeps
into his thoughts.

I try to save pieces of his memory,
tuck them into the folds of time,
but the pain of his unraveling is a weight
straining against my hands,
his mind an ocean through my fingers.

His sadness breaks against me,
a wave that shatters the ground,
pulling me into the tangle of confusion

that has attached itself to all the hours of his days,
each moment eclipsed by the next.

Agitation clouds his expression.
His memories are slipping away.
I become the silence
as he disappears.

THE ART OF WAITING

I learned the art of waiting
when I was thirteen,
when the language of scalpels and disease
invaded the heart of my childhood home.
I folded silently
into the sounds of suffering,
a fixture on cancer wards.

I became acquainted with crowded waiting rooms,
echoes of pain escaping bleached walls,
while doctors sliced tumors
out of my mother's breast.
5 years later,
I stared at the same walls,
withering chips of paint peeling like skin
onto the floor,
as I waited for her to die.

Decades later,
my mother torn to whispers
that sank with the sun beneath the earth,
sorrow still clinging to my bones,
I paced familiar hospital corridors,
waiting to hear if my brother's cancer had spread.

Hours into days into years,
surrounded by the smell of sickness

Today, I watch my father disappear,
wheeled down a stark hallway,
a foreign body invading his bladder.
I wait under the glare of hospital lights,
closing my eyes against memories
that remind me how heavy sadness can be.
He doesn't know my name,
but I will be here when he wakes up.

PRISTINE

She was tall but not willowy,
legs like twigs,
ankles that fought against the wind.
She was obsessed with her teeth.
Twice a month, she boarded a train
to New York,
bound for a world of dental hygiene
and men wielding melodious drills.
She kept a toothbrush in her purse
to clean her teeth after every meal,
flossed with vigor and avoided sweets,
determined to defy the imminent death
of her incisors.
Her best dresses stayed pressed and
crisp in her closet,
saved for dental excursions and funerals.
Most days she was mean,
bitterness dictating the scowl on her face,
but every month, on those two days,
you were guaranteed to see her smile.
Her mouth was pristine.

STAIN

I see myself through your prickly lens.

A stain on the family crest,
hiding in the mouth of a shadow
to obscure the shame that comes
with being ugly.

An uncomfortable silence
lingering like a bad smell,
shit on a shoe that just won't budge.

I am the one who was never supposed to breathe,
the deformity in an otherwise
perfect batch.

I slice myself out of photographs,
cover the dullness of my skin
with petals bruised by clumsy fingers,
and trick my eyes
with the burn of whiskey,
straight up.

I am a wish made on a candle with no wick,
the scar on a canvass

painted over, covered up.
The one who never belonged inside the frame.

My name sullies the page,
burns through the symmetry of straight teeth
and long blonde hair.

I strike a match against the fabric of conformity,
memorize the shapes of weapons
you keep hidden behind your teeth.

I become a pinprick of rage,
hiding in the corner of your eye,
waiting patiently for you to stumble,
to fall.

I am the one you never suspected,
the one who will stand over the crumbling
bones of your ego,
throw off my mask of contrition
and leave you to choke on my words.

THE DRUNK

I step into a spiral
the dregs of cabernet in my mouth
float
for a moment
sink
kiss the blur of oblivion

I am a seamstress
a weaver of the temporary
disappearing act
an angel with a slick tongue

a drunk

My mirror image
distorts under the bite of gin
dirty and smoky in the glass
I am suspended
fleeting
beautiful

I am a devil
masquerading beneath silken fingers
a seductress with tripwires

on the edges of her teeth

a drunk

I stagger onto a path of delusions
flooding my mouth
with the sweet burn of whiskey
to numb the fall

I am a whisper tethered tightly
to the hand of addiction
eyes closed
a shallow breath in a blackout

a drunk

CHOREOGRAPHED

He was an older boy,
the first to put his fingers inside me,
to kiss me with longing,
tongue grazing my innocence
like the lip of a flame.
He was mine for a season,
love caught up in the hands of danger and drugs,
but I was made of glass
and wouldn't let him break me.

With the demise of leaves marking the end of autumn,
he moved on to more experienced girls,
girls who put out, but evaded the moniker of slut
by wearing their sadness on the inside.
He flashed smiles and slipped beneath their skirts,
but couldn't erase the whisper of me from his skin.
I became something for him to conquer,
to hold in the warmth of his mouth.

I choreographed our first fuck,
the burn of winter and cheap bourbon on my tongue.
We met under the moon,
got a little drunk to loosen our nerves,
made out for an hour in the woods.

Shivering, as the snow fell around us,

I took his hand and led him through a hidden door,

down into the basement of the girl's dormitory.

I remember the dim light

welcoming us in from the cold,

the dusty mattress on the floor.

I remember he put his jacket beneath me,

his teenage version of chivalry,

but I can't remember how it felt,

if it was any good.

I was only 15.

COLOR DISAPPEARS

This morning, orange disappeared.

The glare of daylight brings darkness,

a flash that cleans slate and wipes color

from every surface.

I learn to rely on the clicks of heater gauges,

the labored breath of the chase.

I run,

flat out,

as fast as my thick and aging legs

will carry me.

I am caught every time,

the net widening,

the pitch black of midnight seeping

into the cracks of the sun.

Today, orange disappeared,

became shadows and ravens and fear.

Tomorrow may be the last time I ever see green.

STILL ALIVE

I find my father wandering the halls,
his daily search for an escape.
He sees me, and tears flood his eyes.
"I thought you had been killed,"
he tells me.

"No, Dad,
I am fine.
I am sorry you were scared."
Tears still fall from his eyes,
but now they fall in shades of relief.

"When is your brother coming?"
he asks
"John will be here soon, Dad."
My brother has been dead for 6 years

"Is Allan still alive?"
my father asks me.
"Yes, Dad,
you are".

GRIEF

(part one)

Torn by emptiness
My breath falters in silence
The taste of light fades

(part two)

I hold onto grief
Weave it into my bruised skin
My bones turn to ash

IN THE MOUTH OF A WARM WIND

I wish I could disappear,

vapor into the mouth of a warm wind.

I want to be swallowed by a mist

that swirls into the air,

so thick my eyes become an ocean.

I dream I can climb beneath the water,

where the quiet feeds me

and washes away the clamor of time.

I wish I could sleep so deeply

I would forget the touch of sadness,

slip behind the eyes of the moon

and wake up in a new skin.

PAPER BONES

I punch in the code for the second floor,
elevator slowly ascending to a locked ward.
A secret space
for those whose minds have pulled up roots,
memory twisting and evaporating
like petals floating into the clutches
of an unexpected wind.

I see him.
My father,
paper bones rattling beneath his skin,
tiny frame swallowed up
by the beige cushions of a chair.
I watch him,
fingers entwined with those of the woman beside him.

She strokes circles into the back of his hand,
her thumb soothing a patchwork of weary veins,
silently,
as if the room around them never existed.
They stare into each other's eyes,
speaking a language filled with shapes and pathways
that traverse beneath a sky
only they can touch.

A clatter of plates pulls him from their connection.

He sees me,

watching him,

a spectator on the edges of his new reality.

His eyes blink the room into focus.

He lifts his hand as if it holds the weight of the sun,

reaches for me.

Today, he knows I am his daughter.

SWIMMING THROUGH TUNNELS

The surface of the pool shimmers with secrets I am hesitant to discover, taunting me with what may be hiding in its depths. I haven't strayed this close to the water's edge in fourteen years. Not since before my diagnosis. I venture in slowly, water lapping at my ankles, caressing the backs of my knees. I feel four years old again, excited, fearful. I descend slowly, toes hesitating on the cool concrete, until I reach the precipice of the final step and sink into the silence. Beneath the water, my eyes transform the pool into a narrow passageway, watery walls that enclose me with gentle hands. I feel oddly comforted, as if, beneath the water, I am truly alone. I wonder if this is what it feels like to drown, to disappear. I hold my breath and swim into the mouth of the tunnel, into the darkness. I cover the length of the pool in seconds, coming up for air when my fingers graze a sand- papery wall. I dive down again and again, abandoning myself to the sensation of peace that comes with being wrapped in the tunnel's watery embrace. For years, I have been bombarded with the term "tunnel vision" as a description of my blindness, felt terrified to experience its claustrophobic grip, to feel the sensations of its true meaning. Today, in the pool, my first time swimming blind, I finally understand. The water has given me clarity. I am no longer afraid.

PERPETUAL LIGHT AND MOTION

He opens his eyes,
feels time creep along his back.
The ache is only temporary.

Music drifts in from the kitchen,
his daughter singing,
calling him to rise into the day.
He hears his wife laughing
and rushes to see what he has missed,
eager to feel the warmth of them.

They are the light that pours through clouds,
watercolor summers that breathe so deeply
the days seem to stand still.

I asked him once,
"How are your gorgeous girls?"
"Flying"
he told me.
I thought of the sky,
days in perpetual light and motion.
I imagined he must always feel so warm,
living in the palm of the sun.

SLIPPING BENEATH TIME

If I slip beneath time, race back to seventeen,
will you stay with me,
spreading poppies on the wind with your laugh,
singing me awake on birthday mornings.
If I smudge out history, pluck the weeds
that death scattered between twenty and thirty,
will you save me,
pull me from the bottom of a bottle,
shatter it against the sky.
If I step into the sun, turn willingly toward fifty,
will you see me,
youth pouring over my fingertips
as the light is wiped from my eyes.

THE LEAVES OF A HUNDRED TREES

Forty-three years ago
our father drove down a quiet street
lush with the leaves of a hundred trees,
and found the house of his dreams,
a haven of silence behind bricks and mortar.
On weekends, he communed with the earth,
planting his heart in rich soil that gave birth
to the fragrant colors of summer,
and constructed homes for wayward birds
beneath a sky that held the sun so gently,
it never burned.

When he died, the house grew cold,
bones cracking without the weight of his hands
to soothe and mend.
Flowers perished and trees wept leaves.
His wife's children snuck in like terror birds
risen from extinction,
foraging for scraps.
They bloodied bridges and assembled bombs
from shards of legal rhetoric,
barricaded the doors and locked us out.

Like schoolyard bullies,
they beat on hollow chests that echoed
with the colorless thrum of cruelty,
and declared themselves victorious.
They pulled threads from a web of deception
tangled in their mother's teeth,
and stitched our mouths shut
with words meant to muzzle and intimidate.
We watched them retreat,
egos heavy with the bravado of victory,
backs turned on those they believed fallen,
but they had forgotten who we are.

We are the leaves of a hundred trees,
his heart planted in the earth,
the fragrant colors of summer,
the sky that holds the sun so gently,
it never burns.
We are our father's daughters.

PIERCING THE MOON

You are the slice of bone

That pierces the moon

The light behind my eye

Reminding me I was loved

I dreamt you were the night sky

Watching over me

Sprinkling stardust on my cheeks

To soften the weight of my tears

When they lowered you into the ground

I knew the earth could never keep you

Buried in darkness

Tethered to its roots

You were always meant to fly

ROSE WATER

Critics say I write too much of darkness,

step too easily into waves of sorrow.

So few see the side of me that blooms in color.

Close your eyes.

Listen.

The colors will come alive

like the heartbeat tick

of the clock.

If you touch me like I am made of paper,

thin and lined and blank,

my scars will melt away,

youth stretching its gossamer fingers to the surface.

I will become the first poem you ever read,

the verse of a song that touches your lips

again and again.

If I fashion my final resting place from petals,

play you music that sits in your blood

like a first kiss,

the fragrance of these words may linger,

a drop of rose water

stashed away delicately on the back of your tongue.

People who shine too brightly
fade into shallow skies.
I am a dim light,
a warm mouth you can ease into,
a whisper that slips inside you gently.
Before you know it,
I have swallowed your heart.

HAND STITCHED

Under the precision of a steel blade,
her youth is carved into a gilded shell,
identity scripted into her throat.
She trades her soul
for sculpted cheekbones
and expertly crafted slices of beauty,
her undesirable bits left like
scraps in a hazardous waste bucket.
Rage is pinned to the roof of her mouth,
trapped behind shellacked lips,
glamour painted into her eyes.
She never blinks.
She is cut into fragments then pieced together,
hand-stitched with bits of plastic
that stick to her ribs and
keep her motionless under hot lights.
She tries to speak,
but her tongue has been plucked out.
Perfection has no sound.

DEVOTION

They are a habit of grave consequence,
a rivalry unraveling on papery skin
ravaged by addiction to victory.
The tension between them slices bitterness
into the wind, undercurrents sharpened
by decades of vigorous competition
and the fight for control.

Vanity becomes the blood that feeds rage.
Arsenals of weapons incubate on their tongues,
igniting into battles that lacerate egos
and leave the kind of scars that never fade.
The devotion to suffering binds them,
stitched by an insatiable need to be the best.
A patchwork of incisions they carry with pride.

For forty years they tally their victories,
displaying them with arrogance,
and bear the weight of defeat with spite.
Their insults become brittle and break,
splintering against the brutality of time,
but still, they lash out and rise to the fight.
There is always one more chance to win.

PLUCK AND SLIP

She shames my father,
interrogates him as if he is a child
caught breaking the rules.
The resentment in her voice
bites down on the air.
She wipes the music from his lips,
choking the notes of his joy
with a grip that freezes the sun,
until he disappears
beneath the weight of her punishing.

Her voice crawls into my ears
like an ache that won't dull,
the pluck and slip of her tongue
wrapping malice into the air.
Sadness twists into my belly,
blooms,
travels into my chest,
expands in my throat.
A storm rages in my mouth,
grinding against my clenched jaw.

Cruelty turns her words into barbs
that puncture my father's heart,

her mean streak slicing
into the rice paper of his memory.
I want to shout and shake her,
make her understand that value doesn't live
in remembering a name.
She can't see the shades of light
still alive in his eyes.

BRANDING IRON

My eyes are held captive by a battalion
of defective genes that creep
along the perimeter of my visual field,
winding tightly around
the delicate palette of my retinas.
I am the plaything of a disease that eats the sun.

Blindness is my constant companion.
It beats against my eyelids without respite,
fracturing my sight with slivers of obsidian.
I see the world through shrinking tunnels,
pinpricks of light smudged
by the punishing fingers of faulty DNA.

I grasp desperately for the last beams of light
that trickle through the cracks,
the bones of my confidence breaking
as the ground is pulled into the mouths of shadows.
The branding iron of genetic mutation
scars darkness into the sky,
extinguishing the shape of my hands.

SCATTERING INTO THE SKY

I pull a chair close to his bed,
steel legs trapping the edges of a starched
white sheet,
and watch him breathing.
The room is warm,
fever pushing through his thin skin,
pressing against my eyes.
It is the end,
the curtain slowing fading,
falling.
The air is hushed,
as if already in mourning.

His gasps echo through the room,
a portent
shattering the ceiling.
His fingers are restless,
lost.
I wait for him to reach out one last time,
but there is nothing to pluck from the air,
only stillness now,

seeping in between each feverish breath,
pulse slowly scattering into the sky.

I lean in,
my lips soft against his cheek,
and whisper,
"nothing to do now but fly."

THE LAST MOMENTS OF DAYLIGHT

She lingers on a park bench,
holding tightly to a splintering cane,
knuckles burgeoning with arthritis.
The tattered collar of a black wool coat
scratches her frail neck.
Peering through the last moments
of daylight catching on the bite
of an Autumn breeze,
she captures me in the root of her eye.
She has a story to tell.
Her whisper strikes the sky,
unfurling images of her childhood,
shattered by a plague of malice
born in the blood of a mad man.
She wrings memories of fear
into the papery skin of her hands,
swollen with the echo of seasons buried
beneath cinders of bone and genocide.
The blood of death marches stains her feet,
slaughter and carnage etched into her skin.
She has swallowed despair,

throat scarred by an unyielding grip of terror,

silenced by the threat of a soldier's gun.

Time is scorched by shadows.

Tears smudge her milky eyes,

as she struggles to break through

the ashes of a world

she believes will never stop burning.

KAT

We met as drops of chaos on the wind,
anguish chasing us through
high school corridors,
exploring skyways to soothe the ache.

She is onyx threads and scarlet outlines,
emeralds that capture light through clouds.
I am the fist of the storm,
sapphires and black cat's eye scapolite.
Together we conquer shadows.

She is a seamstress
weaving magic through printed sound.
Lifetimes unravel from her fingertips,
falling like music,
lush
onto the page.

I am a conjurer of snapshots
that incarcerate slices of time,
heartbreak held tightly
like a jewel
in the center of my palm.

The years have changed the shape
of our hearts,
stolen the soft texture of our skin,
but the roots of our friendship tether us.
We are sisters in light and darkness.

PRIMROSE MELTING

Leaves burst into flame, doused in peril and
painting dread into days that cease to linger.
I watch the end of a burning, when the ash
has turned cold and lays like a shroud on the
carcasses of leaves, red veins dormant.

A canopy carved from icicles darkens
weary bones entombed beneath a sheath of snow.
Stillness seeps into the landscape and hushes the sky,
filling the bitter hours of twilight with slumber.
Dreams are echoes that punctuate the silence.

The aching limbs of fields rise like the dead,
pushing roots through the pulse of the soil.
The ground erupts in a clamor of sprouting emeralds.
Trees sigh beneath the weight of new life,
a veil of blossoms wrapping the branches in splendor.

Primrose and inhibitions melt, gleaming on asphalt.
Blades of grass lay frail and broken under
the gaze of fiery eyes that burn without respite.
A heatwave blisters the countryside,
sputters with a final breath,
and climbs into Autumn's chilling mouth.

ALONE IN A ROOM WITH MY FATHER AND DEATH

I sit with my father

Alone

Death peering over his shoulder

He doesn't speak

We both barely breathe

Waiting

He has been bathed by a nurse

Dressed in a navy- blue shirt I bought for him

It's almost brand new

Collar crisp

Buttons undone

to make room for the struggling pulse at his throat

His hair is thick and white

Still beautiful

Cut and combed into perfect formation

His eyes are closed

Mouth open

in a plea for one more taste of air

He pulls a breath into his lungs

ten seconds

twenty

thirty

forty

Each time he stops breathing

I stop breathing with him

SYCAMORE LEAVES

Fog rolled in the day we buried you,
sorrow twisting around cherry wood,
seeping into the disrupted soil.
The rain followed in its wake.
Emptiness resonated in the cool drops
that dampened my black wool dress,
striking the delicate bones beneath my eyes
as you were lowered into the ground.

You were happiest when the mist thickened
the air, and the streets of our beachside town
vanished into the obscurity of its shroud.
On stormy days, after school, you greeted us
with pots of earl grey and a fire the crackled
against the walls of our small stone hearth.
It seemed only right that it rained the morning
the earth pulled you into its maze of roots and bone.

A year before you died, torn by the teeth
of chemotherapy, writhing in agony
on long car rides to the emergency room,
you begged for death, pleading with god
to make the suffering stop.
You predicted the cancer would stretch

its fingers into your blood, curling like
vines around your diminishing breath.

On good days, when the pain loosened its grip,
and the sun slipped back into your bones,
you searched in secret for a final resting place.
You chose a site nestled under the heavy
branches of a sycamore tree,
leaves weeping over the epitaph carved
into the black marble of your gravestone,
promising we could always find you.

FLUTTER

There is a flutter in my thumb,
a red-winged blackbird struggling
against my pulse,
harbinger of a storm brewing
in the center of my chest.
Her carnelian wings shatter against my ribcage,
the shape of my heart forever altered.

There is a shadow in my eye,
a raven that fills my head with nightmares,
blocking out the sun with shrieks of calamity.
I reach into the darkening sky,
try to pull light back into my mouth.
I have forgotten who I was before fear
crept under my skin.

There is a wishbone in my throat.
a sparrow quietly singing,
all hope of resurrection
caught in the marrow of a lilting refrain.
She reminds me I was once alive,
whispers, it is ok to open your eyes,
to find the voice you lost that day in the rain.

THE EDGE OF A STAR

Yesterday I spent too much time
under the hum of florescent lights,
in the company of a back-lit screen
and an eagerness to find the right words.

The morning delivers my sentence,
with barbed patches of daylight
that puncture my retinas like an anvil
fresh from the fire.
My day has been molded
by the fingers of a genetic mutation.

To the untrained eye,
I careen like water down the street,
a ghost on the scarred pavement
cocooning my city.
A large brimmed hat and sunglasses
hide my affliction,
eyes sealed shut against the shrieking sun.
I leave my cane at home,
wanting to blend in,
to feel normal.

I carry a secret at the back of my eye.

Disease has turned me into the calamity
that stumbles across a dimly lit room,
outstretched hands bruised,
hips colliding with table corners.
I drop and spill out over the midnight floor.
Darkness travels like a bullet
through my blood,
plucking clarity from the walls,
tearing the light out of my eyes.

I am a shadow that wraps itself
around the moon,
a cluster of clouds
heavy with the threat of a storm.
Tumbling from the edge of a star,
I bleed into the night sky
as it becomes invisible.

Susan Richardson

THE SECRET TO FOLDING LAUNDRY

When I am alone,

folding crisp white shirts and faded sheets

that once held the scent of lavender,

I am a dancer

grazing the worn wood of the apartment floor,

a feather on the wind,

weightless,

at ease.

In the center of this loneliness,

I shed my heavy skin,

wash away the darkening circles of blindness.

I am a tall tree

with leaves so gentle,

even the angriest storms pass me by.

In the notes I find courage,

a stranger,

a woman who opens herself like a star.

I become the whole sky.

Swept up in a song,

the noise of my disease is canceled and quelled.

When he comes home, the laundry is folded.

My secret is safe.

PUZZLE PIECES

He died in a single bed
that swallowed up his withering limbs,
cradled in white sheets that never had time
to hold his scent,
surrounded by beige walls
scarred by the blood of a thousand nails.
When he moved into the facility,
we brought puzzle pieces of his life
to hang on the walls
and help him remember.
Pictures of his first two kids,
the ones with promise,
the ones he wanted.
A drawing of Freud looking obstinate,
mischief lurking beneath his beard,
a mirror image of my father.
And, a small painting of an owl,
eyes smudged out by time,
feathers nestled into its body to protect it from pain.
It hangs on my wall now.

SOMETIMES STRANGERS ARE BREAKABLE

I stand in the center of a dim room, motionless, avoiding the mirror and what I have allowed myself to become, a grotesque reminder of loss that pushes at the seams of my skin and hides the frailty of my heart. Sometimes it feels as if my bones will shatter under all this weight, breaking me into shards of shame that slice open the fabric of my identity. I hold my breath and raise my eyes to the reflection of a stranger. Her face is withering, held together by the threads of a wraith, the wings of youth stretching and breaking against the blades of time. I am crushed by shadows, memories that pluck the sleep from my eyes. Am I awake? This cannot possibly be a dream, this pain that pushes me down into the darkness. It is luxurious, this descent, this drowning. I can't feel myself breathing, but for a moment, I think I hear the stranger in the mirror laughing. I watch her weightless body shake with sensations that are unfamiliar. I have a fleeting desire to stop and acquaint myself with her, but I cannot be distracted from my sinking.

CACTUS GARDEN

You were tall, with an unruly beard
and strong hands.
I was twenty-seven, with a head full of darkness
and a dead mother.
The first time I saw you, your face awash in stillness
and what I mistook for disdain,
I was afraid to be alone with you.
Then you spoke and I disappeared like vapor
into the rhythm of your voice.
You talked about art and poetry,
your god
and your wife.
It was the day we became friends.

I waited for the hours when we worked together,
barely breathing in my car
on the commute to work,
listening to music you had recommended,
driving too fast.
I watched you counting out change,
your hands calloused from hours holding a
paintbrush.
I stood a little too close, smiled a little too long,
found opportunities to touch you,

fingers lingering on your arm.
I imagined longing in your eyes.
But it was faith.

Your god shielded you from the kind of betrayal
that grows out of forbidden feelings,
but desire was alive on my tongue,
in the curve of my mouth,
longing to be satiated.
I craved the weight of your hands,
covered in paint,
touching me without regret,
as if I were made of canvass.

On Wednesday afternoons we had lunch together,
explored the grounds of the museum
hunting for treasure and serenity.
I fell in love with you
under the gaze of a cactus garden,
ensconced in a veil of needles,
alone in a distant corner of our
stone and steel maze.
I imagined you were mine,
but fantasies crack
and girls filled with darkness stumble.
I began to dismantle my life,
frayed the threads of our friendship

to keep my secret safe.

I shouted at you once,
called you self-righteous, a liar,
used the hurt in your eyes against you.
For months we didn't speak.
On lonely lunch breaks, filled with silence,
I wept and searched
for the solace of our cactus garden,
nestled at the edge of the world
where danger felt like magic,
and I could be alone with my feelings for you.

We reconciled at a work party,
under stars that sparkled against the travertine.
You smiled at me and held your wife's hand.
I wanted to stay and be warmed by your voice,
take in the milk of your words,
but I left too quickly,
afraid of a jealous girlfriend
who forbade me from talking to you.
That night, she pushed me down a flight of stairs.

As I tumbled over the wooden steps,
I thought of your gentle hands
and the shadowy figures
that appeared like angels in your paintings.

I thought of our friendship,
how I had missed you,
how I had always loved you.
I landed at the bottom of the stairs,
rose up from the darkness and fled the shackles
that had bound me to crushing fists
and bouts of rage.
I never told you,
but that was the night you saved my life.

THE WALTZ

We drape ourselves in the haberdashery
of tragic life and cook up schemes that
splinter against faltering panes of reality.
Waltzing over a precipice,
we fall like whispers into a chasm of defiance,
escaping the ravenous warnings that threaten
to devour our fantasy.
Cradled in the comradery of self -deception,
we feed our blood with bottles of wine
to smooth the scars that traverse across our hearts.
We creep like sleuths over the backs of shadows
and hide behind veils of glass
to avoid the guillotine of sober living.
I curl with pleasure into your hands,
inhale the comforting textures of solidarity.
A history of loss spackles your palms,
stories I have read a thousand times,
pages dog eared and washed in the scent of tenderness.
From the roots of my own nightmare,
I reach for your voice
falling like water over the edges of my eyes.
Light and sound disappear into your mouth.

BLUE BIRD

When his mind started to fade,
my father made me promise to feed him to the fire,
to set his body free.
Two weeks after he died,
my husband and I drove through rush hour,
wind creaking through the bones
of our old forest green pickup truck,
an engagement present from my father
when he still knew my name.
We drove in silence
to collect what the flames had left behind.

In the parking lot of the cremation center,
I held my husband's hand,
reluctant to step through the doors.
Loose coins rattled against a spice jar
hidden in my purse,
watery crystal from an import shop.
Something to hold a piece of him,
until we could plant the ashes in a garden
that wasn't yet ours.

We were greeted in a dimly lit room
by a young man with eager eyes and dark hair

pressed into place with sticky gel.

He spoke softly

gently

but still, it startled me.

"Did you bring an urn?"

My breath caught behind my teeth,

fingers hesitating against the spice jar.

A woman wearing heavy black glasses

that framed the condolence in her eyes,

led us down a hallway so quiet,

I could almost hear the grief that lingered

in the soft brown fibers of carpet.

We followed her over footfalls of sorrow,

into an office with three blank walls,

the fourth dressed with a display of urns

and resting containers for loved ones.

On a high shelf I spotted a white bird,

smooth glass wings preparing for flight.

"There is also a blue bird," she said,

pointing to a stormy porcelain figurine

perched beside an urn blooming with painted irises.

"Blue, just like your eyes."

I smiled, tears fresh on my cheeks.

I have my father's eyes.

WHISKEY SOUR

She loses herself in the scent of an arabesque,
gliding en' pointe across
the supple fingers of Tchaikovsky,
and forgets where her life went astray.
20 years of pouring alcohol into the mouths
of men with meandering hands,
choking on the fumes of boozy propositions
and ashtrays that overflow with regret.
She stands at the bar, a pillar of composure,
waiting for bottles of beer to serve up,
last rites to professional drunks.
The curve of her neck is elegant,
almost inviting.
She closes her eyes and disappears
beneath the dim lights,
spinning through the bliss of a perfect pirouette.
Wrapped in the silken fabric of her daydream,
she breaks free from the confines of servitude,
threaded into her hair to satisfy the appetites
of brutes who lay claim to bar stools.
Her tongue covets the grandeur of champagne.
She gets wasted on stolen whiskey sours,
struggling to ignore the seedy stares of pub crawlers,
as her life sinks into a deep plie'.

BETWEEN SIGHT AND BLINDNESS

I play the blind card to shut you up,
skillfully peeling expectation from your tongue,
unleashing the secrets you keep locked in your mouth.
Fantasies that live in the spaces behind your eyes
ignite with the fervor of my fingertips,
expertly seeking out the shapes of your longing.
My lips beckon and burn against your throat.
I entice your hunger with hands adept at feeling
their way across bodies slashed by the bite of desire.
Are you wondering what it feels like to be touched
by a blind woman?

I play the blind card to show you I can see.
I don't need eyes to know when you are lying,
waxing poetic over my mouth as the words
sour the air, wither and rot.
Your voice is saturated in the clamor of deception,
drowning me in an urge to tear sound from the sky.
I conceal my rage in a clenched jaw,
resentment coating my tongue like paraffin.
I become the hunter, ensnare you in the darkness.
Are you curious what it sounds like inside the eye
of a blind woman's fury?

I play the blind card to help you understand.

Clarity lurks in the spaces between sight and blindness.

On a quest for resurrection,

I move freely into spikes of light,

bearing the burden of pain as I offer my vision

into the clutches of disease.

The fragrance of truth washes over my eyelids,

clearing the debris of sedition from my mind.

The sun burns my eyes into ash

that can only give birth in darkness.

I am unbound from the musings

of what blind women see.

RATTLE

Each new loss reminds me of the last,
a puzzle piece that has slipped
out of reach,
a familiar ache
sliced from the periphery of my thoughts.

My father's papery hand,
frail against my swollen salty fingers,
his eyes searching my face,
fighting to see through the fog that consumes his mind
as he tries to remember my name.

My brother,
the rattle of death in his chest as he lay
struggling to breathe,
eyes shut tight against the fear
of what comes next,
or what might not.

My mother's eyes,
a storm that lingered for 3 days,
full of the longing to stay
just a little while longer.
I remember the chill of the rain on my face
the morning that she died.

ORIGAMI

She walks down streets
Searching for glitter
Head tucked
Creases into folds
An origami box
Never crane in flight
Or blooming flower
No dragon fire
No kimono quilt
To cover her pain
The beauty of the city is
Scorched and sharpened
Blades of paper push
Through sidewalk cracks
Slicing shards of confidence
From those who dare
To dream

THE LENGTH OF A MINUTE

I sit beside death,
watch it warping time,
listen to the shallow breath of it.
I can see in the color of his hands
he is fading.
Today dimmer than yesterday.

The length of a minute expands
and holds its breath.
An hour stretches its fingers
through the bones of space
and holds on,
as if the stars depend on touch for sustenance.

My father reaches out,
trying to catch pieces of the sky.
I hold his hand.
"You are safe,"
I tell him,
she can't hurt you now."
"It is ok to say goodbye."

SCORCHED

She hides the sun behind her eyes,
identity bleached
into the threads of a mask
she wears with spite.
Her laugh pours thorough crooked teeth,
sound torn by the blistering
of summer,
scorched and hollow
from the pit of her throat.

She is the cruel end of a knife,
a miscreant steeped in ice,
skin worn almost to the bone.
The elastic of her mind
loosens her tongue.
Insults tumble from the lip of a blade,
slice into emptiness.

She is alone
She has always been alone.

STITCHING BONES

Murmurs of rage constrict my breath,

serpentine flash against the tip of my tongue.

I resign myself to the ache of living in captivity.

Vines of anger cascade over the edges of

pedestals carved from violence and shackle me

to walls covered in the scent of rancor.

I climb into the teeth of misery.

She is a vice that clamps my mouth silent,

turning my words into shards of hatred

that burrow into the back of my throat.

The strike of a serrated refrain

crumbles me into silage,

feeding the roots of an unrelenting noise

that lingers in the hum of my blood.

I sink quietly into the clamor,

stitching my bones with filaments of patience.

One day I will emerge,

armed with a battalion of embers on my tongue,

and incinerate her mocking grin.

CORNER CHILD

I came into the world marked for failure,
hiding my face,
innocence stripped by the expectation
to fix a failing marriage.
I was a corner child,
a keeper of peace
molded tight into the silence,
splinters of an unraveling family
pressed against my eyes.

I have peeled myself away
half a dozen times,
heart like lead
encased in ice.
I slip
unsteady,
into gashes and cracks in the floor,
a hiding place for the damned.
I curl into the brutality
of my own false and feeble protests,
lost beneath the stone.
I sink into these moments,
secret
heavy

dirty.

I sweep the debris of my fuck ups
into piles.
A turret built from pieces of shame.
I dream so vividly
inside the shackles of my fortress,
pressing into its sharp edges.
My hands are still,
poised to keep the pain alive.
I no longer recognize myself
outside these walls.

STONES OF UNKNOWN ORIGIN

My youth is steeped in the smell of terminal illness.
It settles in the fabric of my mother's favorite blanket,
consuming me with images of her suffering.
Emptiness feeds an ache that stains my fingertips,
tangled in threads that slice into the light.
My hands carry the scars of a childhood
dedicated to grief.

I stumble into thirty,
searching for someone to cure my loneliness.
An elixir of lies clouds my judgment,
dulling the scent of betrayal on her lips.
I climb into the bite of her tin foil tongue.
Love is a fabrication that cultivates the roots of regret,
a whisper of duplicity that chokes my desire.
My mouth bears the wounds of deception.

Approaching forty, I peer over the edge of possibility.
I tread cautiously over stones of unknown origin,
searching for the scent of hope
to soften the ground beneath my feet.
His voice falls over my eyes like a talisman,
guiding me across the darkening terrain.
My heart is mended in the safety of his grasp.

PUNCTURE

Tree roots puncture the skin of the sidewalk,
veins of earth slithering
around my ankles,
pulling me to the ground.
Blindness is a trickster with slick fingers,
a smooth tongue
sneaking up the back of my neck,
setting my pulse alight with fear.

I grasp at false idols
images of myself
that exist only beyond borders
that unravel with the strike of time.
How do you bloom from a core that is fractured,
thrive under the gaze of a sun
that bleaches out the textures of the landscape?

My sight scatters into the gullet of the floor,
disappearing into the clutches of shadows,
whispers goodbye in the quiet rise of the moon.
I close my eyes and wait for stars to appear
like diamonds on my lashes.
They never arrive.

SCAVENGER

We are a world apart.

You, a diamond

casting a glow into the darkness.

Me, asleep with a bottle

tucked like treasure

under the shards of a rough blanket.

I followed you down a steep path

carved from golden flecks of promise,

where bright lights consumed you

and left me

to scavenge in your gilded dust.

My hands are brutal and scarred

from the effort.

I try to find traces of you in myself,

wiping my face clean

to erase the mistakes of my flesh,

but dreams like these can only be found

at the bottom of a bottle.

Caught in the clutches of red wine,

hopeful that I have disappeared,

I find my eyes still tangled in a storm,

ravaged by the misfortunes of being

the ugly sister.
I hear the sound of you sparkling,
miles beneath the silence of the sky,
and slip back under the covers
to sleep away another drunken night.

FABRIC OF MADNESS

He is a fixture on my street corner,

blending into the stains of an urban backdrop,

face smudged out by the brutal fist of the sun.

He sits like a bruise on the filthy sidewalk,

muttering and pleading for change

to buy cans of cheap beer.

His knees are scuffed by months of

crawling over pavement,

rummaging for fragments of himself.

He clings to the frayed edges of clarity,

grasping for glimmers of who he used to be.

The scent of memory brushes against his eyelids,

wavering in a frame that flickers and fades,

fingers of silk, soft against his striking chin,

tongue slipping carelessly into snifters of brandy.

His identity is a murmur,

a snapshot buried deep in the fabric of his mind.

He forgets his name as he sinks into madness,

pulling sorrow and rotting breath

from the strands of his brittle beard.

WHEN I THINK OF LEONARD COHEN

I think of blow jobs on unmade beds,
birthmarks and Berlin and what ticks
like a bomb
underneath the noise of the river.
I think of his lush locks of hair
and being touched by sadness,
fingers moving like an ache
across my thighs.

Desperation thrives
beneath dirty hotel sheets,
dangerous,
cut off from the act of breathing,
of consequences.

He would have fucked me when I was 25,
maybe even looked into my eyes,
made me coffee
while falling in love with my poetry,
the grit of it,
the dirty underbelly of it,
the despair.

When I think of you,
I think of beauty,
of all the strange in-between spaces
that entice us into the arms of strangers.
I think that maybe,
just maybe,
you would have been compelled to touch me
for an hour,
to fall in love with the odd curves of my face,
the frailty of my heart.

Now I am 50,
heart filled with gravel,
unfuckable.

THE LIFE AND DEATH OF A LOVE AFFAIR

I was hollow then
Before your skin and rhythm
Branded my twilight

In those first moments
Hands shaking and cautious heart
I tasted a dream

Your words are like wind
Sweetly they chill to the bone
Go straight to my head

Pressed against the dawn
Full of promise and smooth mist
We never step out

I feel our stories
Entangled imperfections
Resting on thin ice

The truth falls brightly

Sun shining on its burnt stem
Swiftly we descend

Generous with masks
You come and dash like pepper
Your excuse sits still

Nightfall grows frigid
Wrapped in the arms of your lies
Your absence heavy

When you disappear
You grasp your pastel clad bitch
Under an old sheet

Indecision rules
Your yes is tentative, gray
I hang by your thread

Just one more life left
We have used up eight of ours
Live this one softly

Cruel slips of your tongue
Twist, strangle, suffocate me

You fade too quickly

I am empty now
Without your chaos and light
To spark my senses

SMUDGE

I sneak around the edges of my reflection
desperate to uncover the vestiges of youth
wishing away time and sorrow

My eyes are an assault of loneliness
a storm that smudges out hope

Darkness winds itself into the light

The facade of my thirties is lost
vanished into deep purple grooves
hidden beneath weakening skin

My mouth is slivered with disgust
a taste that chokes my longing

Defeat winds itself into my tongue

I am a stranger in a body tricked by time
trapped under the thumb of over-indulgence
greedy cheeks stuffed with denial

My chin bears the burden of this face
ugly before it ever grew old

Disappointment winds itself around my neck

I BELONGED TO YOU

You called me a waif, admonishing me for
exploring the neighborhood in bare feet,
soles blackened by suburban soot.
With tender hands and a smile that
edged away the undertow of frustration,
you washed the blood from my stubbed toes
and bandaged the wounds
of a stalwart and reckless childhood.
Your rage burned out of control for the other kids,
but I was the child of your reinvention,
a story that found its voice in the waves.

I have his eyes, but I belonged to you.
It was you who taught me the art of sadness,
washing my tiny hands in the despair of your tears.
You strapped me to your chest
and climbed out of a life steeped in secrecy,
into a decade of feminist rallies
and learning how to roar.
But the weight of your sorrow had stained us both.
You hit me once, when I was six years old.
I hit back.
We sat at the bottom of the steps together and cried.

DARKNESS STRETCHES

The sun rises later every day as October unfolds itself into the imminence of winter. I can't help but watch all the ways in which the darkness stretches, how some kinds of darkness are elusive, others you can touch, and feel deep inside you. But it is fleeting, and like the darkness, I am fleeting, uncertain, trapped beneath the weight of grief. It is as it should be.

On October 7, my father took his last breath, and the sky was overcome with a clamor so quiet, my own breathing felt like an intrusion. His death was a devastation wrapped so peacefully, so gently, in the hands of my sister and myself, as we comforted him through his final rite of passage. I am aching but feel no regret. I miss him but find myself smiling, laughing, remembering how lucky we were to be friends, to be father and daughter. He taught me how to breathe through the process of breaking, gave me poetry to cushion the fall and music as an elixir.

I welcome these darkening mornings, this looking glass into the bones of winter. It is my time to remember, to realize that in the unruly rhythm of my heart, my father lives, as does my mother and my brother. I welcome this sadness, this reflection. I miss him. It is as it should be.

THE WEIGHT OF STARS

I am a pinprick of time blackened by disease,
searching for a reflection of my younger self,
wrinkles smoothed and heart hollowed out.
My hands hold five decades of sorrow.
Liquor pushes pain to the back of my tongue,
a slow burn that pulls me into the roots of escape,
absorbing the emptiness in my chest.
I hold the texture of the sun
in a memory that lives behind my eyes.
My body is a stranger,
a usurper that shatters against the fist of loss.
I am a perishing sky,
sinking into the throat of nightfall.
I hold the ache of stars in my bones,
the weight of them in my belly.

DREAMING OF LOVE

I dream that my teeth are crumbling,

the sun breaking into sparks of silence

that incinerate my tongue.

I dream the sky is tumbling from my mouth,

shapes of azurite

filling the palm of my hand.

I dream of fractures in the moon,

sorrow seeping out from between the cracks,

hope lodged in the marrow.

I dream of your heartbeat,

falling like thunder into my throat.

I dream that I am weightless,

wind.

I dream that I never was.

THE LAST TO CRACK

My shell is the last to crack
I am the last torn from mother's flesh
The first one forgotten

My fingers are the last to touch water
I am the last to inhale the scent of waves
The first pulled under the current

My eyes are the last to taste color
I am the last to witness the sun bleeding onto the moon
The first to see the inside of darkness

My voice is the last to bloom
I am the last to take the fullness of sound into my mouth
The first to be silenced

My feet are the last to sink into the earth
I am the last to be uprooted
The first to step willingly into the sky

Acknowledgments

I want to thank River Dixon for taking a chance on me and for being such a generous champion of my work, for his support and encouragement and for bringing me so graciously into the fold of Potter's Grove Press. It is an honor for me to have my work as part of the beautiful and diverse catalog he is creating. I also want to take this opportunity to thank the incredible writing community I have had the good fortune to become a part of, both on Word Press and Twitter. The generosity and kindness of these communities has helped to build my confidence and given me a new sense of belonging. I want to express my gratitude to Lisa Frank and Steve Denehan, for their friendship and the invaluable critique that helped so many of my poems breathe new life. To Bojana Stojčić for her beautiful words and unyielding support of my work. To Tanya Klein, Suzanne Craig – Whytock and Steve Markesich, for their gentle reading, generosity and friendship. Finally, I want to thank, from the whole of my heart, my best friend Kat, for a lifetime of friendship and love, my sister Kaila for leading with an abundance of sunshine, and my husband Joe, who makes everything possible and brings more joy into my life than I ever could have imagined.

Made in the USA
Middletown, DE
03 July 2020